The Most Up-to-date Pocket Guide to Discover the Hidden Treasures of Guadalajara Culture, Must-See Attraction Sites and Insider Tips for Family, Solo Travellers, Seniors and First-Timers

Guadalajara Travel Guide 2024

ROLAND RICHARD

Table of Contents

Table of Contents 3
Map of Guadalajara 6
Introduction 7
    Welcome to Guadelajara 10
    About This Guide 11
    Why Visit Guadalajara in 2024 11
    Essential Travel Information 11
Chapter 1 13
Planning Your Trip to Guadalajara 13
    Ideal Time to Go 14
    Entry and Visa Requirements 15
    Money and Financial Concerns 16
    Communication 17
    Options for Accommodation 18
Chapter 2 20
Exploring Guadalajara's Culture 20
    A Brief Overview of Guadalajara's Past 20
    Local Traditions and Customs 22
    Arts and Culture Landscape 24
    Events and Festivals 25
Chapter 3 28
Must-See Attractions in Guadalajara 28
    The Historic Centro 29
    The Museums in Guadalajara 30

Copyright 2023. Roland Richard.

All rights Reserved!

No part of this book may be reproduced, stored in a retrieval system, or transmitted in any form or by any means, electronic, mechanical, photocopying, recording, or otherwise, without the prior written permission of the copyright owner.

Stunning Churches and Cathedrals	31
Vibrant Mercados	32
The Tequila Trail	33
Chapter 4	**35**
Guadalajara for Family Travelers	35
Family-Friendly Attractions	35
Child-Friendly Cafes & Restaurants	37
Safety Tips for Family Travel	39
Chapter 5	**41**
Solo Traveler's Guide to Guadalajara	41
Solo Travel Tips	42
Best Places for Solo Explorations	44
Meeting Locals and Other Solo Travelers	45
Chapter 6	**47**
Seniors' Retreat in Guadalajara	47
Senior-Friendly Attractions	48
Safety and Health Issues	49
Mobility and Accessibility	51
Chapter 7	**53**
First-Timer's Guadalajara Itinerary	53
3-Day Itinerary for First-Timers	53
5-Day Itinerary for a Deeper Experience	56
Chapter 8	**58**
Food and Dining in Guadalajara	58
Traditional Mexican Cuisine	58
The Culinary Scene in Guadalajara	61

Restaurants and Dishes You Must Try	62
Chapter 9	**65**
Insider Tips and Local Secrets	65
Tips for Saving Money	65
Hidden Treasures in Guadalajara	66
Local Suggestions	68
Chapter 10	**70**
Getting Around Guadalajara	70
Means of Transportation	71
Finding your way in the City	72
Chapter 11	**75**
Staying Safe in Guadalajara	75
Safety Advice	75
Emergency Numbers	78
Chapter 12	**80**
Beyond Guadalajara	80
Day Trips & Adventures	80
Exploring the Surrounding Areas	83
Conclusion	**87**
Appendix	**89**
Handy Phrases	89
Checklist for Packing	91
Practical Apps & Websites	93
Guadalajara Travel Vocabulary	94
Recommended Reading	96
Guadalajara Road Map	99

Map of Guadalajara

Introduction

As I set out to explore this intriguing Mexican city, the sun was low in the sky, giving Guadalajara a warm, golden colour. Street food vendors were cooking up local specialities, lending a tantalising aroma to the air, while the lively plazas reverberated with the rhythmic playing of mariachi bands. I was drawn farther into Guadalajara's enthralling embrace with every step and sensed the city's rich history and culture.

The contrast between old and new was something I kept thinking about as I strolled around the city's mediaeval streets. The smooth fusion of Guadalajara's modernity and heritage was evident in the silent reverence of gleaming buildings next to centuries-old cathedrals. Surrounded by elaborate colonial buildings that attested to the passage of time, I was in the centre of the Historic Centro.

It was eye-opening to discover the city's cultural gems. Known as the "Mercado San Juan de Dios," the bustling Mercado Libertad was a sensory experience that took me to the heart of Mexican cuisine, while the Instituto Cultural Cabañas, a UNESCO World Heritage Site, captivated me with its magnificent frescoes by José Clemente Orozco.

Through the mesmerising sounds of mariachi music, I was able to travel back in time and experience a whole new side of Guadalajara. The city was a symphony of feelings and tales, with the passion and pride of its inhabitants evident in every note and lyric.

I was greeted with open arms by the people of Guadalajara as I ventured deeper into its colourful tapestry. They shared their beloved customs with me, such as drinking tequila in the middle of agave fields and having wild fiestas with an infectious energy.

Still, time seemed to stand when I left the busy streets of the city and entered the serene embrace of Lake Chapala. Ajijic's small village and its tranquil waters offered a welcome break from the bustle of the metropolis, allowing me to think about the harmony between the two.

Guadalajara was more than just a place I visited; it was a city that welcomed me with open arms, and I felt completely immersed in it. This was an experience with culture, history, and the unwavering spirit of a place that embraced life with contagious zeal.

Upon contemplating my individual experience in Guadalajara, I am reminded that travel is about more than just exploring new locations; it's about developing relationships, making memories, and bringing a little piece of the globe home with you. A treasured chapter in my ever-changing trip through this amazing place, Guadalajara has become a part of my tale thanks to its warm friendliness and diverse encounters.

Welcome to Guadelajara

Welcome to the "Guadalajara Travel Guide 2024," your indispensable travel guide for discovering Guadalajara, a bustling city. The goal of this guide is to give you the most recent details and insider advice to ensure that your trip is unforgettable.

About This Guide

This section will provide you with an idea of the format and how to use the guide. It will assist you in navigating the abundance of information offered to improve your time in Guadalajara.

Why Visit Guadalajara in 2024

Learn about the exceptional events and attractions that will make 2024 a memorable year to visit Guadalajara. This section will provide you with updated information to schedule your vacation for this year, ranging from new developments to cultural festivals.

Essential Travel Information

1. *Visa and Entry Requirements:* Find out what you'll need for your trip to Guadalajara in terms of travel documents and visa requirements.

2. *Currency and Financial Matters:* Acquire knowledge of local money, exchange rates, and useful advice for handling your funds while visiting.
3. *Language and Communication:* Learn Spanish, which is the main language used in Guadalajara, and discover practical ways to communicate with locals to overcome any linguistic obstacles.
4. *Accommodations:* Learn about a variety of lodging options, including hotels and hostels, so you can select the one that best fits your needs and price range.

Chapter 1

Planning Your Trip to Guadalajara

A plethora of cultural riches and engaging experiences await you in the dynamic city of Guadalajara. I'll provide you with useful information in this chapter to help you plan your trip, such as the ideal time to go, visa requirements, currency information, language advice, and lodging possibilities. You'll also be provided with anticipated expenses to help you create a budget.

Ideal Time to Go

The ideal time to visit Guadalajara will depend on your choices as the city's climate has something unique to offer in every season:

★ *Spring in Guadalajara (March to May):* This is a great season to visit. The afternoon highs are in the warm mid-70s to 80s Fahrenheit (21-27°C). There are excellent bargains on lodging, and hotel rates are fair.

★ *Summer (June to August):* Guadalajara experiences milder summers, with typical highs of 80–90°F (27–32°C). Vibrant festivals, including the International Mariachi Festival, are happening this season. Because of the increasing number of tourists, expect higher hotel charges.

★ *Autumn (September to November):* With temperatures between 70 and 80°F (21-27°C), autumn is a nice time to visit. It's a great time to explore without the bustle of the city as the crowds thin out. In general, hotel rates are moderate.

★ *Winter (December to February):* Guadalajara experiences warm winters, with evenings that are colder and daily highs of 70–75°F (21–24°C). It's a more sedate period to visit with fewer visitors, and accommodations are reasonably priced, making it an economical option.

Entry and Visa Requirements

Depending on your country, Guadalajara has different entry and visa requirements. The majority of visitors from the US, Canada, the EU, and many other nations do not need to have a visa to enter Mexico for tourism and may remain for up to 180 days. But your passport needs to be current and have at least six months left on it.

Estimated Visa Cost: The cost of a visa may differ based on your nationality. A tourist visa (FMM) typically costs about $22 for nationals of the United States.

Money and Financial Concerns

The Mexican Peso (MXN) is the accepted form of payment in Guadalajara. The following approximate expenditures will assist you in creating your budget:

- *Meals:* A three-course meal at a mid-range restaurant can cost $20–30 USD, while street food can cost $5–$7.
- *Accommodations:* Rates for hotels differ greatly. While mid-range hotels cost between $50 and $100 per night, hostels can be found for as little as $15 to $30 per night for travellers on a tight budget. Luxurious lodgings can run you $150 or more.
- *Transportation:* Uber is available as well as taxis, which typically start at $3 within the city. Like buses, public

transport is reasonably priced, with most tickets costing less than $1.

- *Entertainment:* Depending on the location, museum and cultural attraction admission prices might range from $2 to $10.

Communication

In Guadalajara, Spanish is the official language. Even though many people in the tourism sector can communicate in some English, it can be more convenient to communicate if you know a few simple Spanish words. It can be helpful to learn words like "hello" (hola), "please" (por favour), and "thank you" (gracias) while communicating with locals.

You can buy a local SIM card or think about getting an international data plan from your provider to keep connected. In Guadalajara, a lot of cafés and hotels provide free WiFi, so you may rely on communication applications for calls and messages as well.

Options for Accommodation

Guadalajara provides a variety of lodging choices to fit different price ranges:

- *Budget:* A night in a hostel or guesthouse might run you as low as $15–30 USD.
- *Mid-Range Hotels:* Estimated cost is from $50 to $100 a night, there are cosy mid-range hotels to choose from.
- *Luxurious Accommodations*: This can set you back $150 or more for those who are looking for it.

Reservations for lodging should be made well in advance, particularly during busy travel periods or significant occasions.

With the necessary trip-planning knowledge and anticipated expenses at your disposal, you can confidently move forward and begin discovering Guadalajara's hidden gems, gastronomic delights, and cultural treasures. I'll make sure you get the most out of your trip by taking you through the centre of this fascinating city in the next chapters.

Guachimontones, Guadalajara

Chapter 2

Exploring Guadalajara's Culture

A Brief Overview of Guadalajara's Past

The fascinating story of Guadalajara's rich past begins with Cristóbal de Oñate's establishment of the city in 1542. This city's distinct personality has been shaped by the rise and fall of civilizations over the ages. Be sure to check out these historical sites when you stroll around Guadalajara:

- *Instituto Cultural Cabañas (Cabañas Cultural Institute):* Instituto Cultural Cabañas, also known as the Cabañas Cultural Institute, is a stunning architectural creation that was first built in the late 1700s as an orphanage. The institute is home to a breathtaking collection of José Clemente Orozco murals and is currently recognised as a UNESCO World Heritage site. These murals, which were finished between 1936 and 1939, portray important themes from Mexican history, justice, and human struggle.
- *Government Palace (Palacio de Gobierno):* José Clemente Orozco murals adorn the Government building (Palacio de Gobierno), a historic building with neoclassical architecture. The paintings, which were made between 1937 and 1939, depict the history of

Mexico, starting with pre-Hispanic cultures and ending with the Mexican Revolution.

- *Teatro Degollado (Degollado Theater):* Built in the middle of the 19th century, the large neoclassical Teatro Degollado (also known as the Degollado Theatre) is a cultural landmark in Guadalajara. It has played a significant role in the history of the city by hosting some noteworthy occasions and performances.

Local Traditions and Customs

Understanding local traditions and manners is crucial if you want to fully immerse yourself in Guadalajara culture:

- *Greetings:* Saying "Hola" or "Buenos días" is the traditional method to start a conversation in Guadalajara. Shaking hands is customary when you first meet someone. It's common for acquaintances to give one other a quick embrace or cheek kiss.

- *Dining manners:* Mexican culture places a high value on dining decorum. Keeping your hands visible on the table with your wrists resting on the edge is considered courteous. Meals usually start as soon as the host gets going. Saying "Buen provecho" to other diners before you eat is polite.
- *Respect for Religion:* The numerous churches and religious celebrations in Guadalajara provide witness to the city's strong Catholic background. Wear modest clothing that covers your knees and shoulders when you visit these locations. It is anticipated that you will speak quietly and with respect.
- *Tipping:* In Guadalajara, leaving a tip is traditional. A gratuity of between 10% and 15% of the entire bill is customary in restaurants for excellent service. In other service contexts, including hotels and cabs, providing a

little gratuity for exceptional service is customarily appreciated.

Arts and Culture Landscape

The vibrant arts and entertainment scene in Guadalajara is a manifestation of Mexican creativity:

- *Murals:* Explore the world of murals, especially the ones at the Hospicio Cabañas painted by José Clemente Orozco. These well-known murals, which were painted between 1936 and 1939, are regarded as some of Orozco's best works and show the hopes and sufferings of the Mexican people.
- *Museums:* Guadalajara is home to a wide variety of museums, each of which provides a distinctive viewpoint on Mexico's creative legacy. Two of the many organisations that let you examine Mexican culture via

the artistic medium are the Museo de Arte de Zapopan and the Museo Regional de Guadalajara.

- *Music and Dancing:* The strains of mariachi bands fill the streets and plazas of Guadalajara, the cradle of mariachi music. Experience the passion and energy of traditional Mexican dancing and music by going to a live mariachi performance.

Events and Festivals

The city of Guadalajara knows how to joyfully celebrate life and culture. Don't pass on these thrilling celebrations and events:

- *International Mariachi Festival (Festival Internacional del Mariachi):* Festival Internacional del Mariachi, often known as the International Mariachi Festival: This festival, which takes place every year in late August or early September, is a vibrant celebration of mariachi music. Take pleasure in parades, concerts, and seeing musicians wearing recognisable charro attire. It's a happy occasion to celebrate Mexican identity.
- *Day of the Dead (Día de los Muertos):* Discover the captivating customs of Día de los Muertos, observed on November 1st and 2nd: Celebrate the Day of the Dead. Take part in processions, observe elaborate ofrendas (altars) honouring departed family members, and

become fully immersed in this distinctive Mexican custom that honours the life-death cycle.

- *International Film Festival (Festival Internacional de Cine en Guadalajara, or FICG):* This well-known event, which takes place in March, attracts movie buffs from all over the world. It's a chance to take in the art and culture of Guadalajara in addition to watching a wide range of foreign and Mexican films.

Every cobblestone street, every artwork, and every festival parade in Guadalajara convey a story of resiliency, inventiveness, and tradition. The city's culture is a live, breathing narrative. Whether you're a history buff, an art enthusiast, or just someone who loves to be happy, Guadalajara's rich cultural diversity will enthral your senses and make a lasting impression on your heart.

Chapter 3

Must-See Attractions in Guadalajara

Visiting Guadalajara's most famous and essential sites would be a must-do when exploring the city's culture. We'll take you through the city's historical district, several museums, beautiful churches and cathedrals, bustling mercados (markets), and the alluring Tequila Trail in this chapter.

The Historic Centro

The Historic Centro, Guadalajara's beating heart, is a mesmerising fusion of culture, history, and city life:

★ *Plaza de Armas (GPS: 20.6230° N, 103.2420° W):* The Palacio de Gobierno and the Metropolitan Cathedral are two of the historic structures encircling the main square. It's a fantastic spot to begin your research.

★ *Metropolitan Cathedral (GPS: 20.6236° N, 103.2431° W):* Constructed in the sixteenth century, this imposing church is a masterwork of Spanish colonial design. Enter to see its elaborate interior.

★ *Rotonda de los Jaliscienses Ilustres (GPS: 20.6219° N, 103.2450° W):* The Rotonda de los Jaliscienses Ilustres honours the most illustrious residents of Jalisco. The life tales of famous Jaliscans are depicted in the statues and plaques.

★ *Hospicio Cabañas (GPS: 20.6712° N, 103.3523° W):* Known for the breathtaking murals by José Clemente Orozco, this former orphanage is recognised as a UNESCO World Heritage site. The murals, which feature the "Man of Fire" motif, are a must-see for art lovers.

The Museums in Guadalajara

For those who love art and history, Guadalajara is a paradise. Check out these top-notch museums:

★ *Museo Regional de Guadalajara (GPS: 20.6223° N, 103.2494° W):* The Museo Regional de Guadalajara has an amazing collection of artefacts, including pre-Hispanic antiquities, colonial art, and modern shows, that will help you discover the rich history of Jalisco and Mexico.

★ *Museo de Arte de Zapopan (GPS: 20.7221° N, 103.3835° W):* This museum, which is situated in the city of Zapopan, has a wide range of modern and contemporary artwork, including pieces by well-known Mexican painters.

★ *Museo Trompo Mágico (GPS: 20.6627° N, 103.4023° W) :* This interactive children's museum is ideal for families as it provides engaging experiences, informative programmes, and hands-on displays for kids of all ages.

Stunning Churches and Cathedrals

The religious architecture of Guadalajara bears witness to the city's rich religious heritage:

★ *Guadalajara Cathedral (GPS: 20.6238° N, 103.2439° W):* With its twin towers and exquisite altars, this church is a magnificent example of Spanish colonial architecture. Reach the summit for sweeping city views.

★ *Basílica de Zapopan (GPS: 20.7207° N, 103.4127° W):* The Basilica de Zapopan, situated in the nearby city of Zapopan, is a noteworthy religious location that is well-known for its highly esteemed statue of the Virgin of Zapopan.

Vibrant Mercados

The marketplaces in Guadalajara are a visual feast, with everything from regional food to handcrafted goods:

★ *Mercado Libertad (San Juan de Dios Market) (GPS: 20.6765° N, 103.3525° W):* One of the biggest indoor marketplaces in Latin America is the Mercado Libertad, also known as the San Juan de Dios Market. It is a lively place to shop. It is a veritable gold mine of regional specialities, apparel, and handicrafts. Don't forget to sample the well-known regional delicacy birria.

★ *Mercado de Abastos (GPS: 20.6839° N, 103.3090° W):* Guadalajara's wholesale market offers an intriguing window into the local cuisine. Various fresh food, spices and local favourites are available.

The Tequila Trail

The Tequila Trail takes travellers through the heart of the tequila sector if they have an adventurous spirit:

★ *Tequila Town (GPS: 20.8823° N, 103.8230° W):* Discover the origins of Tequila, the most well-known spirit in Mexico, by visiting Tequila Town. See distilleries and discover how tequila is made. You will love it!

★ *Agave Fields:* Wander through the agave fields, which are home to the well-known blue agave plants that are cultivated and harvested for tequila.

★ *Tequila Tastings:* Sample various tequila variabilities and discover the distinctive flavours and characteristics that set each apart.

The historical, cultural, and gastronomic attractions of Guadalajara are a must-see, and you'll be enthralled by the city's diverse experiences. These attractions capture the spirit of Guadalajara, whether you're strolling around the historic centre, viewing art at museums, or enjoying tequila on the Tequila Trail.

The Tequila Trail

Chapter 4

Guadalajara for Family Travelers

Are you visiting Guadalajara with your family? With a wealth of family-friendly sights, lovely kid-friendly restaurants, and crucial safety advice, this chapter serves as your guide to an easy and worry-free trip throughout the city.

Family-Friendly Attractions

Adventurers of all ages can discover a wide range of family-friendly attractions in Guadalajara.

★ *Selva Mágica Amusement Park (GPS: 20.6352° N, 103.3705° W):* Selva Mágica provides both children and adults with an unforgettable experience that includes thrilling rides, live entertainment, and an atmosphere of pure delight.

★ *Guadalajara Zoo (Zoológico Guadalajara) (GPS: 20.6980° N, 103.3717° W):* The Guadalajara Zoo (Zoológico Guadalajara) is a vast zoo that offers an enthralling voyage through the animal kingdom. The whole family will enjoy this fascinating and enlightening trip.

★ *Parque Metropolitano (GPS: 20.6577° N, 103.3920° W):* This huge metropolitan park offers a haven for those who enjoy being outside. It has playgrounds, walking trails, and open areas, making it the perfect place for a picnic with the family or a day of fun activities.

★ *Children's Museum (Museo Trompo Mágico) (GPS: 20.6627° N, 103.4023° W):* A children's wonderland of discovery. The museum is adorned with Interactive displays that pique interest and inspire creativity, turning learning into an enjoyable experience.

★ *Plaza Tapatía (GPS: 20.6230° N, 103.2420° W):* Tucked away in the centre of the city, Plaza Tapatía is a vibrant public space where families can take in street shows, a wide variety of food vendors, and the vibrant atmosphere of Guadalajara.

Child-Friendly Cafes & Restaurants

Finding mouthwatering restaurants that are kid-friendly in Guadalajara is a delight:

★ *Tacos Kids Guadalajara GPS: 20.6663° N, 103.3925° W):* Tacos Kids Guadalajara is a family-friendly restaurant that is well-known for its delicious tacos and a separate space for kids to play, making for a fun meal for all.

★ *La Gorda Sushi and Sashimi Kids (GPS: 20.7235° N, 103.3405° W):* For families looking for a fun sushi experience, this restaurant's kid-friendly menu and relaxed vibe are ideal.

★ *La Antigua (La Antigua Paletería) (GPS: 20.6939° N, 103.3464° W):* This quaint location offers classic Mexican ice creams and paletas (popsicles) that delight adults and children alike.

★ *Pizza Amore (GPS: 20.6595° N, 103.3512° W):* Pizza Amore is well-known for its delicious pizzas that are sure to please even the pickiest palates.

Safety Tips for Family Travel

When visiting Guadalajara, it is crucial to make sure your family is secure and comfortable:

- *Health precautions:* Keep a small first-aid kit on hand in case of minor illnesses or injuries. Make sure everyone has access to plenty of water and sunscreen to shield them from the sun's harmful rays.
- *Stay Together:* It's important to watch out for your kids when you're in crowded areas. To facilitate a speedy reunion if someone is separated, specify a specific meeting place.
- *Transportation Safety:* Make sure you pick reliable companies while using ridesharing or taxis. When

making a taxi reservation, ask for a car seat for little children.

- *Language:* Knowing a few fundamental Spanish words and phrases can be quite beneficial, particularly when asking for help or directions. It is frequently well welcomed when an attempt is made to communicate in the native tongue.

- *Emergency Numbers:* Contact numbers for emergencies should always be readily hand. In Mexico, the standard emergency number is 911. In addition, make sure you have the contact details for the embassy or consulate of your nation in Guadalajara in case you want assistance.

With a variety of attractions, food options, and security precautions to guarantee a happy and safe stay, Guadalajara is a warm and inviting place for families.

Chapter 5

Solo Traveler's Guide to Guadalajara

Guadalajara is a city of opportunities for solo travellers, full of exciting adventures and a rich cultural heritage. This chapter serves as your guide when travelling alone across the city, providing you with important advice, recommendations for solitary exploring spots, and ideas for interacting with residents and other travellers.

Solo Travel Tips

Solo travel is an exciting experience, and Guadalajara extends a warm welcome to those who choose to go it alone. Here are some pointers to guarantee an exciting and secure adventure:

- *Learn Some Basic Spanish Phrases:* Even though most people in the area understand English, knowing a few basic Spanish phrases will help you communicate with the locals and have a better experience.
- *Stay in Well-Reviewed Lodging:* Pick lodgings that are well-regarded for their safety and friendliness to single travellers. Guesthouses, boutique hotels, and hostels are excellent places to meet other travellers.

- *Explore During the Day:* Although Guadalajara is generally secure for visitors, it is still preferable to explore during the day, particularly if you are travelling alone. This is true of any city.
- *Use Reputable Transportation:* When travelling, stick to reputable ride-sharing applications like Uber or taxi services. Always make a note of the driver's details and give them to a reliable person.
- *Blend In:* Try to blend in by wearing modestly and staying away from expensive or gaudy jewellery and devices to reduce unwelcome attention.
- *Local Food:* Guadalajara is well known for its mouthwatering cuisine. Visit neighbourhood restaurants and food stands to enjoy real Mexican food; you might even start a discussion with other patrons.
- *Be Open to New Experiences:* Whether it's participating in a neighbourhood festival, sampling an unusual street cuisine, or going to a cultural event, embrace

spontaneity and say "yes" to chances to experience something new.

Best Places for Solo Explorations

There are several areas in Guadalajara to explore on your own:

★ *Tlaquepaque:* A quaint neighbourhood well-known for its stores, traditional crafts, and art galleries. Explore the galleries, stroll around the cobblestone streets, and buy locally made trinkets.

★ *Chapultepec Avenue (Avenida Chapultepec):* A vibrant entertainment centre, Chapultepec Avenue (Avenida Chapultepec) is home to cafes, bars, restaurants, and cultural events. It's a fantastic spot to meet other tourists and residents.

★ *Bosque Colomos (Colomos Forest):* The tranquil urban park known as Bosque Colomos, or Colomos Forest, features lush vegetation and strolling paths. It's the perfect place for a solitary nature escape.

★ *Galleries and Museums:* Guadalajara is home to numerous art galleries where you may learn about the local art scene, as well as the Instituto Cultural Cabañas, which is home to Orozco's murals.

★ *Local marketplaces:* Visit marketplaces such as Mercado Libertad (San Juan de Dios Market) and Mercado de Abastos to fully immerse yourself in the culture. These vibrant markets provide a genuine experience of Guadalajara's daily existence.

Meeting Locals and Other Solo Travelers

One of the pleasures of travelling alone is making connections with locals and other solo travellers:

- *Meetups for Language Exchange:* Search Guadalajara for events or gatherings that involve language exchange.

They are an excellent method to meet people from the area who are keen to learn English and practise Spanish.

- *Cultural Workshops:* A variety of locations in Guadalajara provide workshops in the arts such as cuisine or dance. Engaging in these activities might be a great opportunity to socialise with locals.
- *Attend Festivals and Events:* Keep an eye out for festivals, concerts, and cultural events by checking the local event calendar. These events provide great chances to connect with like-minded individuals.

Guadalajara offers a wealth of cultural activities, delectable food, and chances to interact with friendly locals, making solo travel an exciting trip. If you follow these pointers and approach Guadalajara with an open mind, travelling alone should be a fulfilling and remarkable experience.

Chapter 6

Seniors' Retreat in Guadalajara

Travellers of all ages are welcome in Guadalajara, even elderly people looking for a laid-back yet exciting getaway. To guarantee a relaxing and pleasurable stay in Guadalajara, this chapter includes information about senior-friendly attractions, health and safety issues, and transportation options.

Senior-Friendly Attractions

Seniors can tour Guadalajara's many sights at their leisure.

★ *Hospicio Cabañas:* Hospicio Cabañas is a UNESCO World Heritage site renowned for the breathtaking murals created by José Clemente Orozco. The hospice offers an engrossing tour of Mexican art and history and provides wheelchair accessibility.

★ *Guadalajara Cathedral (Catedral Basílica de la Asunción de María):* Constructed in the sixteenth century, this architectural marvel is easily accessible and has elaborate altars that make it the ideal place for a quiet visit.

★ *Parque Metropolitano:* This urban park is perfect for seniors looking for strolls or picnics since it has walking routes, serene green spaces, and a laid-back atmosphere.

★ *Guadalajara's Botanical Garden (Jardín Botánico de Guadalajara):* This accessible garden features a diverse range of plants and animals. For those who love the outdoors, it's a peaceful haven.

★ *Plaza de Armas:* This city centre square is ideal for leisurely people-watching while revelling in the lively ambience of the city,

Safety and Health Issues

Even though Guadalajara is a generally secure city, it's important to take health and safety considerations into account, particularly for elderly travellers:

1. **Stay Hydrated:** It can get hot and dry in Guadalajara, so drink plenty of water. Keep a reusable water bottle

with you and drink enough of water throughout the day.

2. **Sun Protection:** Use sunscreen, sunglasses, and a wide-brimmed hat to shield yourself from the sun. If at all possible, try to stay indoors during the hottest parts of the day.

3. **Health precautions:** Make sure you have a small first-aid kit, a copy of your medical documents, and any essential prescriptions. Additionally, getting travel insurance is advised.

4. **Transportation:** To get around, use reliable ride-sharing applications like Uber or taxi services. Verify the driver's identity and provide a reliable contact with the details of your ride.

5. **Walking Safety:** Use caution when crossing streets or pavements that are uneven. For maximum movement, use supportive and comfortable shoes.

Mobility and Accessibility

Guadalajara is progressively becoming more senior traveler-friendly:

1. **Public Transportation:** Buses are part of Guadalajara's public transportation system, although they might not always be the most convenient choice for elderly people. Seek bus routes that have ramps and low floors.

2. **Taxi Services:** Taxis are a practical form of transportation that can be found throughout the city. For increased security and comfort, it's best to use trustworthy ride-sharing applications or taxi services.

3. **Sidewalks and Ramps:** The city has upgraded its walkways and ramps to make many areas more accessible. Nonetheless, it's wise to choose routes that are recognised to be senior-friendly.

4. **Accessible Accommodations:** When making reservations, think about asking for rooms with

amenities that can accommodate elders or those that are wheelchair accessible.

5. **Medical Facilities:** There are several hospitals and medical facilities in Guadalajara, some of which are well-equipped to meet the demands of tourists. In case of an emergency, make sure you have access to medical care.

Seniors are drawn to Guadalajara by its inviting atmosphere, easily accessible attractions, and rich cultural heritage. Senior visitors can enjoy a calm and satisfying stay in this quaint Mexican city by taking into account health and safety issues as well as transit alternatives.

Chapter 7

First-Timer's Guadalajara Itinerary

The fascinating city of Guadalajara offers a plethora of activities just waiting to be explored. For first-time visitors, this chapter offers two different itineraries: a 3-day itinerary that gives you a taste of the city's highlights and a longer 5-day itinerary that allows you to explore the city in greater detail.

3-Day Itinerary for First-Timers

Day 1: Timeless Charm

- **Morning:** Start at the Historic Centro, which is the city's centre. See the Metropolitan Cathedral and Plaza de Armas. The Rotonda de los Jaliscienses Ilustres is a must-see.

- **Lunch:** Visit a nearby restaurant in the Historic Centro to indulge in authentic Mexican food.
- **Afternoon:** Visit Hospicio Cabañas, an architectural marvel featuring murals by Orozco. Explore this UNESCO World Heritage site during the afternoon.
- **Evening:** Take a stroll through Plaza Tapatía in the evening to take in street entertainment, eat at a traditional restaurant, and learn about local culture.

Day 2: Culture and Art

- **Morning:** Visit the Museo Regional de Guadalajara in the morning. Discover the rich past of Mexico and Jalisco by looking through this amazing collection of artefacts.
- **Lunch:** Visit a nearby restaurant and indulge in local cuisine.
- **Afternoon:** Visit the Zapopan city's Museo de Arte de Zapopan. Take in the modern and contemporary art.

➢ **Evening:** Have dinner at a cosy neighbourhood eatery, then if you're interested, check out Chapultepec Avenue's nightlife.

Day 3: Local Flavours and a Day Trip

➢ **Morning:** Spend a day visiting Tequila Town, the cradle of Mexico's famous tequila. Take a tour of agave farms, see distilleries and sample tequila.

➢ **Lunch:** In Tequila Town, savour authentic Mexican food.

➢ **Afternoon:** Go back to Guadalajara and spend some time browsing the San Juan de Dios Market (Mercado Libertad) for some great street cuisine and locally made items.

➢ **Evening:** Enjoy a lavish meal at a neighbourhood restaurant on your final night in Guadalajara.

5-Day Itinerary for a Deeper Experience

Day 4: Relaxation and the outdoors

- **Morning:** Visit the peaceful urban park Bosque Colomos to start your day. Go for a stroll or just unwind in the great outdoors.
- **Lunch:** Have a relaxing meal at a restaurant close to Bosque Colomos.
- **Afternoon:** Visit the Guadalajara Botanical Garden in the afternoon. Savour the peace of this verdant haven as you explore the variety of plants and animals.
- **Evening:** Make your way back to your lodging for a peaceful evening.

Day 5: Nightlife and Local Markets

- **Morning:** Visit the Mercado de Abastos to get a taste of the local way of life. Here, you may peruse fresh produce markets and learn about the city's culinary traditions.

- **Lunch:** Pick a neighbouring eatery or savour regional fare in the Mercado.
- **Afternoon:** Visit Tlaquepaque, a quaint neighbourhood well-known for its boutique stores and art galleries, to continue your research.
- **Evening:** Take advantage of Chapultepec Avenue's vibrant nightlife, which includes a wide variety of eateries, bars, and cultural events. Savour your final evening in the city.

A more thorough exploration of Guadalajara's culture, scenery, and gastronomic delights is provided with this 5-day itinerary. Guadalajara offers something for every kind of tourist, whether you have three or five days to spend there, making your first trip there rewarding and unforgettable.

Chapter 8

Food and Dining in Guadalajara

With a thriving modern dining scene and a diverse array of traditional Mexican foods, Guadalajara is a culinary haven. We will explore authentic Mexican food, and the city's culinary scene, and expose you to must-try foods and eateries that will entice your palate in this chapter.

Traditional Mexican Cuisine

Mexican food is renowned around the world for its strong tastes, large variety of ingredients, and lengthy history. You can enjoy a variety of traditional foods in Guadalajara, such as:

★ *Birria:* A tasty stew served with corn tortillas that is typically made with goat or beef and cooked with a mixture of spices. Taste it at Birrieria Las 9 Esquinas, a beloved local restaurant.

Birria

★ *Tortas Ahogadas:* A speciality of Guadalajara is the "drowned sandwiches" known as tortas ahogadas. They are made of a type of bread called birote that has been packed with beef or pork and covered in a hot tomato sauce. One well-liked location to eat them is La Torta Ahogada El Chino.

- ★ *Pozole:* A filling soup made with chicken or pork with hominy, which is dried maize kernels. Lime, cabbage, and radishes are common garnishes. Pozole from El Charco de las Ranas is well-known.
- ★ *Tamales:* Encased in maize husks or banana leaves, these delectable packages of masa (dough) are stuffed with a variety of fillings. Tamale Poncho is a popular place to enjoy them.
- ★ *Sopes:* Thin, little tortillas topped with meat, lettuce, refried beans, and additional ingredients. A well-liked place to try sopes is El Abajeño.

The Culinary Scene in Guadalajara

Guadalajara's culinary culture provides a variety of international cuisines, fusion dining, and contemporary takes on traditional recipes in addition to traditional Mexican fare. The city is a centre for fine dining establishments as well as street food. Make sure you look into:

★ *Chapultepec Avenue (Avenida Chapultepec):* A variety of cafes, restaurants, bars and food trucks along this bustling thoroughfare. It is an international mashup of flavours.

★ *Zona Rosa:* This posh neighbourhood is home to many expensive restaurants serving fine Mexican and other cuisines.

★ *Mercado Libertad (San Juan de Dios Market):* San Juan de Dios Market, also known as Mercado Libertad, is a culinary journey unto itself. Food vendors there sell both local specialities and classic Mexican street food.

Restaurants and Dishes You Must Try

Find the greatest places to eat in Guadalajara:

★ *La Chata:* Known for its flavorful pozole and birria, this restaurant is a staple of traditional Mexican cuisine.

La Chatta

★ *Hueso:* A unique eating experience with a bone motif across the entire restaurant. The menu features creative Mexican food.

★ *Lula Bistro:* Modern eatery Lula Bistro is well-known for its tasting menus that highlight Mexican ingredients and flavours while adding contemporary touches.

★ *Karne Garibaldi:* Carne en su jugo (meat in its juice) is served in large servings at Karne Garibaldi, a restaurant renowned for having the fastest service in the world.

★ *Lalo!:* Cocina de Barrio: A quaint eatery in a warm and inviting atmosphere that features a menu of Mexican street food.

★ *Tacos Kids Guadalajara:* Tacos Kids Guadalajara is a family-friendly restaurant that serves mouthwatering tacos that are ideal for a real street food experience.

★ *Alcalde:* A fine-dining treasure renowned for its inventive Mexican fare and excellent mezcal and tequila collection.

You can relish creative cuisine, discover classic Mexican specialities, and indulge in delicious street food in Guadalajara's diverse culinary scene. The city offers a wide variety of food and dining alternatives that will satisfy any kind of eater, from gourmets to casual diners.

Karne Garibaldi

Chapter 9

Insider Tips and Local Secrets

Discover Guadalajara's hidden gems by using these insider insights and local knowledge. This chapter will improve your trip experience in this charming city, from cost-cutting tips to finding hidden treasures and insider recommendations.

Tips for Saving Money

- *Use Public Transportation:* The public transportation system in Guadalajara is reasonably priced. Use the buses or light rail to get around the city quickly.
- *Combo Tickets:* A lot of attractions sell discounted combo tickets for visiting several locations. Keep an eye out for these offers.

- *Free Cultural Events:* Look for free cultural events, such as festivals, concerts, and art exhibits, on the local event calendar.
- *Street Food:* Delicious and reasonably priced Mexican food is sold by street vendors. Taste delicious tortas, tamales, and tacos at a fraction of the price of restaurants.
- *Visit Markets:* Guadalajara's markets offer excellent, reasonably priced dining and shopping options. Look around Mercado Libertad to find regional foods and gifts.

Hidden Treasures in Guadalajara

★ *MUSA (Museo de las Artes):* The Museo de las Artes, or MUSA, is a little-known but excellent museum in the Historic Centro. It is housed in a magnificent colonial structure that hosts exhibitions of contemporary art.

★ *Expiatorio Plaza:* Explore the tranquil Colonia Lafayette neighbourhood's Expiatorio Plaza. Enjoy a peaceful diversion from the busy city while taking in the breathtaking views of the Expiatorio Church.

★ *Rincon de los Colomos:* Tucked away in the Colomos Forest, this quaint park serves as a sanctuary inside the city. It offers a tranquil natural retreat with walking trails and a charming lake.

★ *Parque Agua Azul:* Known for its blue-tiled fountains, this urban park is a picturesque location where residents congregate for leisurely walks.

★ *Teatro Degollado:* This neoclassical theatre is a must-see for its architectural beauty and cultural events, even though it's not exactly a hidden gem.

Local Suggestions

★ *Birria Las 9 Esquinas:* Located in the Historic Centro, this restaurant is a local favourite for birria and provides a tasty and genuine experience.

★ *Birrieria Don Boni:* Another well-known birria place that is well-liked by the people for its flavorful food.

★ *Tortas Ahogadas "El Güero":* Known for its authentic Guadalajara speciality, these tortas are served at this well-known eatery.

★ *Café Boutique La Talavera:* Coffee and pastries are served at this quaint café, which has a lovely atmosphere.

★ *Tlaquepaque:* Well-known for its arts and crafts and exciting cultural events, Tlaquepaque is a place that local artists and artisans frequently suggest visiting.

★ *Las Nueve Esquinas (The Nine Corners):* The Nine Corners, or Las Nueve Esquinas, is a lovely neighbourhood with a blend of traditional and modern culture, as well as little streets and local markets.

★ *Plaza Tapatía:* A popular local hangout in the Historic Centro is Plaza Tapatía. This lively public square offers a taste of real Guadalajara life together with street acts and delectable street cuisine.

Plaza Tapatía

Chapter 10

Getting Around Guadalajara

There is plenty to discover in the vibrant city of Guadalajara. This chapter will go over the many forms of transport that are available and provide tips on how to get around the city like a pro.

Means of Transportation

1. *Light Rail (Tren Ligero):* Guadalajara's light rail system, known as the Tron Ligero, is a productive means of transportation throughout the city. It links many communities and important landmarks. For simple access, make sure you get a contactless card.
2. *Buses:* The city offers a comprehensive and reasonably priced bus system. You may go to a variety of locations via buses, but be prepared and seek guidance from locals as routes and schedules can be confusing.
3. *Taxis:* The city has plenty of taxis accessible. To enhance convenience and safety, seek out licenced taxi stands or utilise ride-sharing applications such as Uber.
4. *Bicycle Rentals:* Bicycles are available in several of Guadalajara's neighbourhoods. To see the city at your speed, you can rent bicycles at several locations.

5. *Walking:* One of the finest ways to see Guadalajara's lively streets and culture is by foot, as the city centre is designed with pedestrians in mind. Just be aware of oncoming cars when you're crossing the street.
6. *Car Rentals:* Rental cars are an alternative if you want to travel outside of the city centre. But be ready for difficulties when driving because traffic can get backed up.

Finding your way in the City

1. *GPS and maps:* Use smartphone GPS apps or download offline maps. This will assist you with getting around the city, identifying points of interest, and preventing getting lost. You have also been provided GPS coordinates in this guide to assist you with navigating seamlessly in this vibrant city.
2. *Learn Basic Spanish Phrases:* A few basic Spanish phrases will come in very handy, especially when asking

locals for directions or assistance. While there will be some English speakers in tourist areas, it is still advisable to acquire a few.

3. *Street Addresses:* The neighbourhoods and street numbers in Guadalajara are referred to as colonias. To move around efficiently, become familiar with the names of the streets and the neighbourhoods.

4. *Crosswalk Safety Tip:* Cars don't always abide by pedestrian crosswalks. Wait for the right moment to cross most securely.

5. *Traffic Conditions:* Guadalajara experiences significant traffic during rush hour; therefore, to prevent getting delayed in traffic, schedule your outings properly. This is super important!

6. *Local Tip:* Never be afraid to ask people in the area for advice or directions. Guadalajara locals are renowned for being amiable and eager to help guests. You will find people who are willing to help you navigate easily.

7. *Safety:* Guadalajara is a secure city overall, but it's still a good idea to remain alert and take safety measures, such as securing all your valuables and staying in adequately illuminated places at night.

8. *Wander Around:* It's better to explore the city's Historic Centro on foot. When exploring the historical landmarks, plazas, and hidden gems, wear comfortable shoes and take your time.

9. *Public transit Cards:* For convenience, if you intend to use the buses and light trains regularly, you might want to get a public transit card.

The information in this section, if followed, will help you navigate Guadalajara's streets with confidence and ease so you can discover all of the city's many attractions and charms.

The city begs to be explored!

Chapter 11

Staying Safe in Guadalajara

Although Guadalajara is a reasonably safe city, like with any urban area, it's vital to be mindful of your surroundings and take safety precautions to guarantee a worry-free and secure vacation. We offer safety advice and crucial emergency numbers in this chapter to ensure your safety while visiting Guadalajara.

Safety Advice

1. **Stay Up to Date:** Find out the most recent Guadalajara travel advisories and safety updates before your trip. Your first line of defence is knowledge.
2. **Select Reputable Accommodations:** Look for hotels or guesthouses in secure neighbourhoods with good reviews. To determine how safe and comfortable your

stay will be, read through visitor evaluations. You can feel safe in these reputable hotels;

   a. Hotel Demetria
   b. Hilton Guadalajara
   c. Holiday Inn Select Guadalajara Expo
   d. One Guadalajara Expo:
   e. Hostel Hospedarte Centro
   f. Hotel Morales Historical & Colonial Downtown Core

3. **Travel Insurance:** If you want to travel, you should think about getting insurance that covers medical emergencies, trip cancellations, and lost or stolen luggage.

4. **Keep Valuables Secure:** Passports, cash, and vital documents should be carried in a money belt or covert pouch. Use caution when showcasing pricey devices like cameras or utilising your phone.

5. **Blend In:** To reduce unwanted attention, dress modestly and stay away from expensive or showy jewellery and clothing.
6. **Stay in Well-Lit places:** When night-exploring the city, stay on well-lit streets and steer clear of deserted places.
7. **Walk-in Groups:** Especially at night, try to experience the city with a group or another traveller.
8. **Keep an Eye on Your belongings:** In public areas, exercise caution when handling your luggage and possessions. Public transit and crowded places are potential targets for thieves.
9. **Emergency Contact Plan:** Make sure someone knows where you are at all times by setting up regular check-ins and sharing your trip plan with a trusted acquaintance.
10. **Use Licenced cabs:** When utilising cabs, pick trustworthy and registered companies. If needed, confirm the driver's identity.

11. **Emergency Services:** Learn the locations of the closest police stations, hospitals, and embassies/consulates of your nation.

Emergency Numbers

Here are important phone numbers to have on hand in case of an emergency in Guadalajara:

1. *Emergency Services (Fire, Police, Medical):* In the event of a crime, accident, or medical emergency, dial 911 for rapid assistance.
2. *Tourist Police:* To aid visitors, Guadalajara maintains a dedicated tourist police squad. They can assist and give information in English. Their number is +52 33 3030 4599.
3. *Medical Assistance:* You can reach the Green Cross (Cruz Verde) at +52 33 3615 9827 or the Red Cross

(Cruz Roja) at +52 33 3818 4111 in case of an emergency.

4. *Embassy or Consulate:* Be aware of the phone number and address of your nation's embassy or consulate in Guadalajara in case you need help in an emergency or with a passport problem. The official website of your government has the contact information.

5. *Local Police:* 911 is the standard emergency number for Guadalajara's local police. To report a crime or for non-emergency assistance, please contact the municipal police at +52 33 3942 2424.

6. *Tourist Helpline:* For questions and assistance about tourism, call the Jalisco state government's tourist service hotline at +52 33 3585 3159.

Chapter 12

Beyond Guadalajara

Day Trips & Adventures

★ *Tequila Town:* For those who love tequila, a day trip to Tequila, which is only 65 kilometres from Guadalajara, is essential. See the distillation process, take a tour of the agave fields, and sample tequila at well-known distilleries like Jose Cuervo and Herradura. While touring the beautiful town of Tequila, discover the background and cultural significance of this well-known Mexican alcoholic beverage.

★ *Lake Chapala:* A tranquil getaway just a short drive from Guadalajara is Lake Chapala. Nestled along its beaches, the town of Ajijic is a favourite among foreigners because of its diverse assortment of lakeside restaurants serving both traditional Mexican and international cuisine, as well as its lively art scene and scenic lakefront promenade. Enjoy the calm atmosphere of this lakeside treasure, explore art galleries, and take strolls along the malecón.

★ *Tlaquepaque and Tonala:* The nearby towns of Tlaquepaque and Tonala are well-known for their handicrafts. Tlaquepaque is renowned for its beautifully restored old district, where you can peruse fine shops, galleries, and restaurants set around quaint courtyards. On the other hand, Tonala is well-known for its vibrant street markets, especially the large Thursday market where you can purchase textiles, glassware, ceramics, and other items. Explore amazing handcrafted goods and become fully immersed in the artisan culture of the area.

★ *Zapopan:* Within the Guadalajara metropolitan area, Zapopan is a must-visit destination for those who enjoy culture. See the well-known Basilica of Our Lady of

Zapopan, a significant religious location that is home to a highly revered statue of the Mother Mary. Discover the historic district, take a stroll down the scenic Andador del Templo, and eat at neighbourhood eateries that specialise in authentic Mexican fare.

★ *Chapala and Ajijic:* Lake Chapala's peaceful villages of Chapala and Ajijic provide a laid-back ambience that's perfect for a day of strolls and lakeside meals. Ajijic has a vibrant expat community, lots of galleries, and restaurants with an artistic ambience, while Chapala is well-known for its Malecón and charming centre plaza.

★ *Guachimontones:* This archaeological site, which is roughly 90 kilometres from Guadalajara, is home to the unusual circular pyramids constructed by the Teuchitlan people. Discover the region's pre-Columbian past by exploring the intriguing ruins, which include the Great Pyramid. More background information about this ancient culture can be found in the on-site museum.

★ *Mazamitla:* Known as the "Mexican Switzerland" because of its breathtaking natural beauty, Mazamitla is a charming village in the Sierra Madre Mountains. Enjoy the clean mountain air while strolling through verdant pine trees and taking gorgeous trail rides on your horse. The town itself is quaint, with alpine-style architecture, cobblestone streets, and delicious restaurants serving local cuisine.

Exploring the Surrounding Areas

★ *Sierra Madre Occidental:* There are lots of outdoor activity activities in these mountains. This mountain range offers hiking paths, equestrian riding, and birdwatching opportunities among its beautiful forests. With a wide variety of plants and animals to explore, the Sierra Madre Occidental is a paradise for nature lovers.

★ *Copper Canyon (Barrancas del Cobre):* Situated in the state of Chihuahua, the Copper Canyon (Barrancas del Cobre) is a huge network of canyons that surpasses the depth and size of the Grand Canyon. An amazing experience, the Copper Canyon train ride offers outstanding views of the untamed environment, native cultures, and magnificent vistas. Discover the canyon's depths, go to native settlements, and allow yourself to be mesmerised by this area's natural beauties.

★ *Talpa de Allende:* The Basilica of Our Lady of Talpa, a significant Mexican religious monument, is located in this pilgrimage hamlet that is tucked away in the Sierra Madre Mountains. The town is well-known for its holy celebrations and the basilica's spiritual importance. Travellers and pilgrims come to the town to pay their respects and become fully immersed in its sacred legacy.

★ *Pueblos Mágicos:* The environs of Guadalajara are home to numerous Pueblos Mágicos, or "Magical Towns," which are distinguished by their particular charm, heritage, and cultural offers. A glimpse into the heart of Mexico may be found in towns like Tapalpa, Mascota, and San Sebastián del Oeste, which have historic plazas, cobblestone streets, and artisan traditions.

★ *Beaches:* Guadalajara is located inland, yet it is only a few hours' drive to the breathtaking beaches of the Pacific coast. Explore Puerto Vallarta's coastline attractions; it's a well-liked vacation spot because of its golden beaches, water sports, and exciting nightlife. Others are Mazamitla, Barra de Navidad, Manzanillo, Sayulita and Costalegre. These beaches are within a 4-5 hour drive from Guadalajara.

★ *Aguascalientes:* The adjacent state of Aguascalientes has several attractions, including the city itself, which is well-known for its edifices and lively cultural scene. For those who love history, the Cañada de la Virgen archaeological site is a fascinating trip because it offers insights into the indigenous cultures of the area.

Beyond Guadalajara, these day trips and excursions lead to unlimited possibilities. The surrounding surroundings are full of various experiences just waiting to be discovered and enjoyed, whether your interests are in outdoor adventures, natural wonders, or cultural exploration.

Manzanillo beach

Conclusion

I would like to express my sincere appreciation for your decision to discover this fascinating city and its environs as you approach the last chapter of your travel through the Guadalajara Travel Guide. With the help of this guide, I hope you will have the inspiration, knowledge, and useful information needed to make your trip to Guadalajara one to remember.

Every traveller can discover a variety of experiences in Guadalajara thanks to its lively traditions, rich culture, and friendly atmosphere. This city has something for everyone, from the majestic plazas and fine dining to the verdant surroundings and rich cultural heritage. After reading through the chapters of this guide, I hope you've found the local secrets, hidden treasures, and useful advice that will make your trip to Guadalajara even more enjoyable.

Exploring new places is only one aspect of travel; another is making new memories and forming relationships. I hope you will make treasured memories that will last long after you return home as you immerse yourself in Guadalajara's culture, interact with its people, and enjoy its flavours.

Recall that travel is an exploration journey—not just of new locations, but also of oneself. It extends our views, deepens our understanding of the diversity of the globe, and broadens our horizons. I hope you take with you the spirit of this amazing city and the kindness of its people as you say goodbye to Guadalajara.

I cordially encourage you to carry on your global exploration by sharing your Guadalajara experiences, images, and narratives with other tourists. I hope your next travels are just as fulfilling and exciting as your stay in Guadalajara.

Appendix

This chapter serves as a useful reference for important tools and data that will improve your trip to Guadalajara. We've got you covered with everything from helpful phrases to a packing checklist, suggested applications and websites, and access to local maps.

Handy Phrases

Although a lot of people in Guadalajara can communicate in English, it might still be beneficial to know a few fundamental Spanish words to improve your trip and establish a connection with locals. Here are a few helpful words to get you going:

- Hello: Hola (OH-la)
- Good morning: Buenos días (BWAY-nos DEE-as)
- Good afternoon: Buenas tardes (BWAY-nas TAR-des)

- Good evening/night: Buenas noches (BWAY-nas NOH-chays)
- Please: Por favor (por fa-VOR)
- Thank you: Gracias (GRAH-syas)
- You're welcome: De nada (de NA-da)
- Yes: Sí (SEE)
- No: No (NO)
- Excuse me / I'm sorry: Perdón (pair-DON)
- I don't understand: No entiendo (NO en-TIEN-do)
- How much is this?: Cuánto cuesta esto? (KWAHN-to KWAY-sta ES-to?)
- Where is...?: Dónde está...? (DOHN-de ES-ta...?)
- Restroom: Baño (BAH-nyo)
- I need help: Necesito ayuda (ne-SE-see-to a-YOU-da)
- I would like...: Me gustaría... (me goos-ta-REE-a...)
- Can you help me?: Puede ayudarme? (PWAY-de a-you-DAR-me?)
- I'm lost: Estoy perdido/a (es-TOY pair-DEE-do/a)

- Food: Comida (co-MEE-da)
- Water: Agua (AH-gwa)
- Beer: Cerveza (ser-VEY-sa)
- I have allergies: Tengo alergias (TEN-go a-ler-HEE-as)

Checklist for Packing

To assist you in getting ready for your vacation to Guadalajara, here is a brief packing checklist:

1. **Travel documents:** Driver's licence, passport, visa (if needed), travel insurance, and any tickets or reservations that may be required.
2. **Clothes:** Wear clothes appropriate for the weather, comfy walking shoes, swimwear, a light jacket or sweater (evenings can be chilly), and formal wear if you intend to attend formal events or eat at fancy restaurants.

3. **Toiletries:** Sunscreen, bug repellent, travel-sized toiletries, and any prescription drugs.
4. **Electronics:** phone, camera, charger, adaptor, and any additional gadgets you might require.
5. **Travel accessories:** Travel wallet, money belt, bag, and reusable water bottle are examples of accessories you should bring along
6. **Basic medical materials**: including band-aids, painkillers, and any personal prescriptions, should be included in a first-aid pack.
7. **Travel guidebook:** Don't forget to bring a hard copy of this guide
8. **Snacks:** For convenience, a few non-perishable snacks.
9. **Currency:** Some physical cash for emergencies, along with some local money.
10. **Local maps:** Maps showing the surroundings and the city of Guadalajara. Check this guide.

Practical Apps & Websites

The following websites and apps can improve your travel experience:

- **Google Maps:** To travel to Guadalajara without an internet connection, download the offline maps for the city.
- **Duolingo:** Use the language-learning software Duolingo to improve your Spanish.
- **XE Currency Converter:** Monitor currency rates with the XE Currency Converter.
- **Uber:** Uber is helpful for quick and secure city transportation.
- **TripAdvisor:** Look up reviews and suggestions for eateries, sights to see, and lodging.
- **Airbnb:** This app can be useful if you're thinking about staying somewhere else.

- **Guadalajara Tourism Website:** For the most recent details on events and activities, visit Guadalajara's official tourism website.

https://visitguadalajara.com/

Guadalajara Travel Vocabulary

I've put up a list of frequently used Spanish words linked to travel to help you communicate and comprehend the language:

- Travel: Viajar
- City: Ciudad
- Hotel: Hotel
- Restaurant: Restaurante
- Airport: Aeropuerto
- Bus: Autobús
- Taxi: Taxi
- Train: Tren

- Museum: Museo
- Beach: Playa
- Shopping: Compras
- Currency: Moneda
- Ticket: Boleto
- Excursion: Excursión
- Guide: Guía
- Map: Mapa
- Arrival: Llegada
- Departure: Salida
- Language: Idioma
- Food: Comida
- Drink: Bebida
- Water: Agua
- Thank you: Gracias
- Please: Por favor
- Yes: Sí
- No: No

- Open: Abierto
- Closed: Cerrado
- Restroom: Baño
- Help: Ayuda
- Emergency: Emergencia
- I don't understand: No entiendo
- Goodbye: Adiós

Recommended Reading

Check out these suggested reading selections to learn more about the people, places, and histories of Guadalajara, Mexico:

1. Graham Greene's "The Power and the Glory": A beloved story with a Mexican setting, provides an engaging account of the complexity of the nation.

2. Laura Esquivel's magical realism book "Like Water for Chocolate" tells a lovely and captivating tale set in Mexico.
3. Octavio Paz's "The Labyrinth of Solitude" is a perceptive anthology of essays that explores the Mexican mind and society.
4. Fausto Prado's "Guadalajara, en el siglo XIX" is a historical narrative that illuminates the past of the city and describes Guadalajara in the 19th century.
5. Michael D. Coe's book "Mexico: From the Olmecs to the Aztecs" offers a thorough analysis of the country's prehistoric past.
6. "Mexico: A Traveler's Literary Companion" edited by C.M. Mayo: It offers a literary tour of Mexico through a selection of Mexican tales and works.

You can gain a deeper understanding of Guadalajara, Mexico, and its diverse cultural landscape by using these texts. We hope that these literary suggestions will enhance your travel experience even more.

As you get ready to go on your adventure, keep in mind that every trip has the potential to change you. I hope your time exploring Guadalajara is full of wonder, meaningful experiences, and life-long memories. Goodbye, and have a safe journey!

Guadalajara Road Map

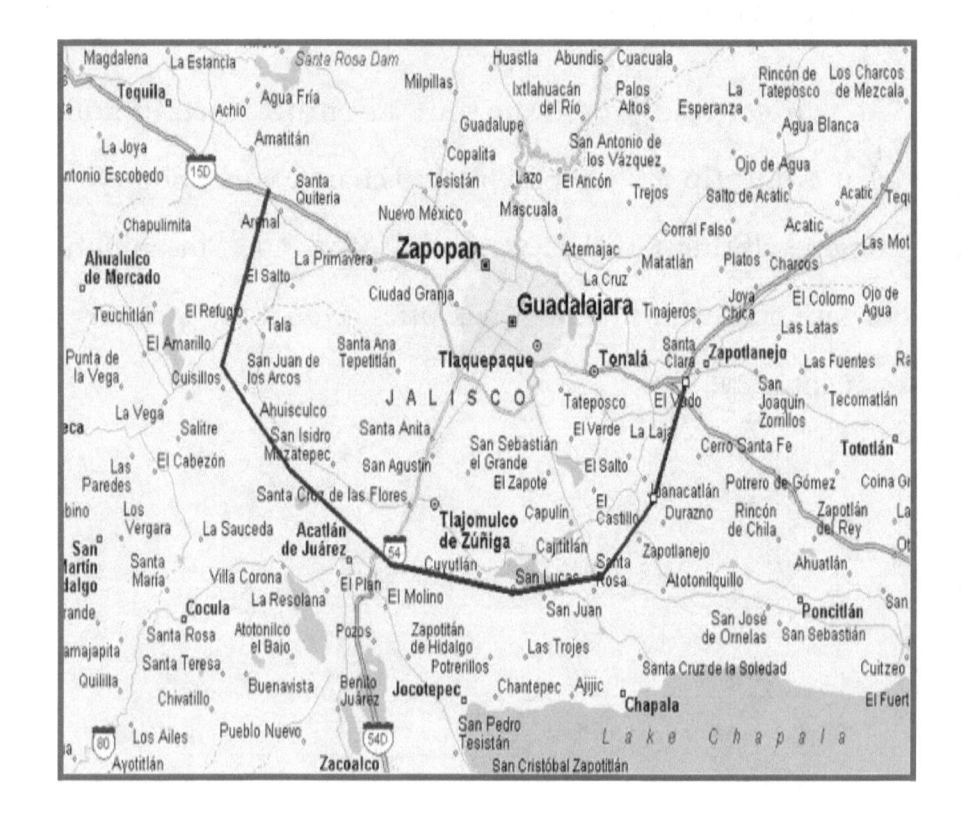

Made in United States
Troutdale, OR
12/04/2024